NORTHLAKE PUBLIC LIBRARY DISTRICT

W9-BTR-224

DATE DUE

	OC 2 8 '97	
MY 27 '95		
JA 18 '96		
JE 22 '96		
JY 24 '98		
OC 8 '98		
MR 28 '98		
OC 5 '98		
AP 14 '99		

CITY OF THE GODS

MEXICO'S ANCIENT CITY OF TEOTIHUACÁN

by Caroline Arnold
Photographs by Richard Hewett

CLARION BOOKS · NEW YORK

NORTHLAKE PUBLIC LIBRARY DISTRICT
231 NORTH WOLF ROAD
NORTHLAKE, ILLINOIS 60164

ACKNOWLEDGMENTS

We thank the National Institute of History and Anthropology of Mexico and the Natural History Museum of Los Angeles County in California for their cooperation in this project. We also give special thanks to Judith Mazari Hiriart and to Carmen García Moreno and her family for all of their help. In addition, we appreciate the assistance of the staff at the Fowler Museum of Cultural History in Los Angeles, California.

Permission to publish the photos on the following pages has been granted by the National Institute of History and Anthropology of Mexico: 1, 4, 6–8, 10, 14, 16, 19, 20, 23, 24, 26, 27, 29–32, 34–44, and the front and back covers.

Clarion Books
a Houghton Mifflin Company imprint
215 Park Avenue South, New York, NY 10003
Text copyright © 1994 by Caroline Arnold
Illustrations copyright © 1994 by Richard Hewett
Text is 14-point Zapf Book Light
Map on page 3 by George Buctel
All rights reserved.
For information about permission to reproduce selections from this book, write to Permissions, Houghton Mifflin Company, 215 Park Avenue South, New York, NY 10003.
Printed in Italy.

Library of Congress Cataloging-in-Publication Data
Arnold, Caroline.
City of the gods: Mexico's ancient city of Teotihuacán/
by Caroline Arnold; photographs by Richard Hewett.
p. cm.
Includes index.
ISBN 0-395-66584-1
1. Teotihuacán Site (San Juan Teotihuacán, Mexico—Juvenile literature. [1. Teotihuacán Site (San Juan Teotihuacán, Mexico)
2. Indians of Mexico—Antiquities. 3. Mexico—Antiquities.]
I. Hewett, Richard, ill. II. Title.
F1219.1.T27A695   1994
972′.52 — dc20   93-40811
                                                                CIP
                                                                AC

NWI 10 9 8 7 6 5 4 3 2 1

Title page: Reproduction of stone head from the Pyramid of the Feathered Serpent.

J
972.52
ARN

14/95

3/15/95

Bob

3/95

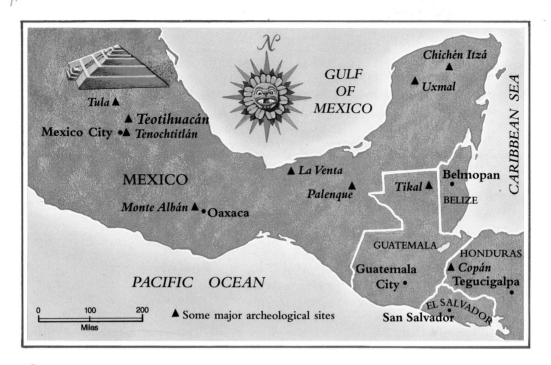

Contents

Exploring the Ruins

On the central plateau of Mexico, just outside the giant modern metropolis of Mexico City, lie the ruins of another great city, the ancient ceremonial complex of Teotihuacán [pronounced Tay-oh-tee-wha-KAHN]. At its center, the enormous 210-foot-high Pyramid of the Sun towers over the city. When it was built nearly 2,000 years ago, priests climbed its 248 steps to worship and study the heavens. Today, the temple that once stood on the pyramid's peak is gone, but, just as the ancient priests once did, visitors can still climb the steps and view the landscape below.

From the top of the Pyramid of the Sun you look down a wide, stone-paved avenue that is bordered by the remains of palaces, temples, and apartment compounds where the people of Teotihuacán lived. To the north, the Pyramid of the Moon rises against the backdrop of the surrounding mountains. To the south are the Citadel, the Pyramid of the Feathered Serpent, the city's administrative center, and a huge plaza that may have been an outdoor market. Beyond the city lies the high, flat plain where the farmers of ancient Teotihuacán once planted their crops.

Pyramid of the Sun.

5

A rich and diverse culture thrived at Teotihuacán long before Europeans came to the Americas. Although the people who built and inhabited the ancient city have been gone for 1,300 years, we can find out about them from what they left behind. The remains of stone and adobe buildings show us where they lived, worked, and worshiped. Sculptures, carvings, and multi-colored paintings help us to learn about their beliefs and customs. Pottery, tools, baskets, jewelry, and other items tell us about their daily lives.

The ruins of Teotihuacán are located 25 miles northeast of Mexico City near the small town of San Juan Teotihuacán. Today they are maintained by the Mexican government as a national archeological site and a place for visitors to learn about life in ancient Mexico. You can see many of the objects that have been discovered at Teotihuacán at the National Museum of Anthropology in Mexico City.

Above: Pyramid of the Moon. Ancient priests studied the moon, planets, and stars and used their knowledge of astronomy and mathematics to make calendars for planting and religious ceremonies.

Below: Colorful murals like this reproduction from the Temple of the Feathered Conches decorated the walls of ancient Teotihuacán.

7

This stone mask, encrusted with turquoise, red shell, mother of pearl, and obsidian, is a masterpiece of Teotihuacán art.

The landscape of Mexico and Central America is rich with the remains of ancient cultures. From around 1500 B.C., when people first established permanent settlements there, to the arrival of Europeans in A.D. 1517, many cultures flourished, including those of the Olmecs, Mayas, Teotihuacános, Toltecs, Aztecs, and others. Each had its own customs, rituals, building styles, and artistic traditions. What distinguishes the culture of Teotihuacán is that it was the first to establish a complex urban center. Archeological research at Teotihuacán is just beginning to reveal the vast scope of this ancient city. As we learn more about the customs and lifestyles of its inhabitants we will gain insights into the development of urban life in the Americas.

The city of Teotihuacán was established around 150 B.C. At the height of its development, between A.D. 300 and 600, it covered an area of eight square miles and had a population of between 100,000 and 200,000 people. But around A.D. 750 a violent revolution destroyed the religious and government structures of Teotihuacán and most of its people left. Although smaller communities developed later on the outskirts of Teotihuacán, the city never regained its former glory. By the fourteenth century, when the Aztec culture began to develop in the region, the life and traditions of the great city of Teotihuacán had long been forgotten.

A huge stone statue of the Great Goddess was discovered in front of the Pyramid of the Moon and is now displayed at the National Museum of Anthropology in Mexico City. It weighs 22 tons and is the largest sculpture ever found at Teotihuacán.

The Aztecs, who are also known as the Mexicas [Me-SHEE-kas], built their capital city, Tenochtitlán [Tay-notch-teet-LAHN], in the place that is now Mexico City. They visited the ruins of Teotihuacán to perform religious ceremonies and created myths to explain how the ancient city had come into being. One story told that Teotihuacán had been built by giants. Another said that it was the birthplace of the Aztec gods.

There is no record of the language spoken by the ancient people of Teotihuacán, so we do not know what they called their city. The name "Teotihuacán" is from the Náhuatl [NA-watl] language spoken by the Aztecs, and means "City of the Gods." All of the place names used at Teotihuacán today are either of Aztec origin or have been given by people who have studied the ruins.

When Spanish explorers came to Mexico in the early 1500s the Aztecs took them to see Teotihuacán. Although some explorations of the ruins were undertaken during the period when Spain governed Mexico, the first scientific studies of Teotihuacán did not begin until the middle of the nineteenth century, after Mexico had achieved independence.

In 1917, an extensive Teotihuacán project was launched by the government of Mexico under the direction of anthropologist Dr. Manuel Gamio. Many of the ruins were excavated and some were restored. Experts made detailed studies of the geography, geology, and plants and animals to better understand how the environment influenced the people of Teotihuacán. They examined objects, paintings, and sculpture to learn about artistic styles and expression. And they studied architecture to learn about ancient building techniques. In recent years, archeologists have made more excavations, drawn detailed maps, and continued to study the thousands of artifacts uncovered by earlier research. Each new discovery helps unlock the secrets of this great culture of long ago.

The high altitude of the valley of Teotihuacán (7,300 to 9,300 feet above sea level) helps make its climate mild.

The Valley of Teotihuacán

The valley of Teotihuacán is part of the central plateau of Mexico, an area of high fertile plains surrounded by mountains and foothills. The climate is semi-dry with most rain falling in the summer. Water is available year round, however, from natural lakes and small streams and rivers that flow down from the mountains.

The first settlers came to the valley of Teotihuacán around 500 B.C. and established small farming villages there. They built irrigation ditches to provide water for their crops and dug the soil with wood and stone tools. Later, as the growing community began to develop into a city, bountiful harvests grown in the rich soil of the valley helped provide food for the increasing population.

Top: Edible cactus fruits are grown at Teotihuacán today just as they were long ago. Middle: Maguey is grown both for its fibers, which are used in textiles, and for its juice, which is made into syrup or fermented to make a drink called pulque.

The ancient farmers of Teotihuacán grew a variety of crops including corn, beans, squash, chiles, tomatoes, and edible cacti. These foods are still part of the traditional diet of Mexico. The people of Teotihuacán also collected wild plants such as potatoes and fruits and hunted rabbits, deer, and other wild animals.

The society of Teotihuacán had a hierarchy of upper and lower classes. The majority of the people belonged to the working class that included farmers, builders, craftspeople, traders, and soldiers. The ruling class was formed by the priests and religious leaders. It is believed that the first rulers of Teotihuacán were powerful religious leaders, and it was under their guidance that the great building program of the pyramids and adjacent temples was begun in the first century A.D.

Bottom: Corn, or maize, was developed as a domestic crop in Mexico more than 7,000 years ago. It was ground into meal on flat grinding stones and then used for cooking. (Pictures of tamales, a kind of steamed corncake, have been found on the walls of apartment compounds at Teotihuacán.)

13

This stone sculpture of a skull surrounded by rays was found in front of the Pyramid of the Sun. The people of Teotihuacán believed that when the sun set in the west, it took its light to the world of the dead.

Religion

Religion was an important part of life for people in ancient Mexico and it was practiced both in the home and at regional ceremonial centers. One of the most ancient ceremonial centers on the central plateau of Mexico was at Cuicuilco [Kwee-KWIL-ko] where there was a temple with a huge circular stone base nearly 500 feet across. Cuicuilco was an important focus of life for the early farmers of Teotihuacán. But in 200 B.C., Cuicuilco was destroyed by the eruption of a volcano. With Cuicuilco gone, Teotihuacán began to develop as the main religious center of the region.

A central belief in the religion of the people of Teotihuacán was that they lived in the place where the world was created and time began. Rituals celebrating this creation myth were believed to promote the continuation of the world and guarantee fertility and prosperity. The exact location of the creation of the world was thought to be a sacred cave. Caves had a special importance for the ancient people of Mexico and Central America, who believed them to be both entrances to and exits from the underworld. Archeologists have found a sacred cave underneath the Pyramid of the Sun. By choosing to build the Pyramid of the Sun over the entrance to this cave, the people of Teotihuacán helped establish the pyramid's religious importance.

Detail of hand and water drops from mural at Tepantitla (Tay-pan-TEET-la).

The religion of Teotihuacán had numerous gods, or deities, each related to a particular aspect of daily life. The most important deity in the Teotihuacán religion was the Great Goddess. Her realm included nature, lakes and rivers, fertility, and caves. She was also associated with the sun. The Great Goddess is always seen facing forward with her face hidden. Her open hands are often shown dispensing water, seeds, or jade and she is sometimes surrounded by lush scenes of plants and animals. In Aztec times, the Great Goddess was called Chalchiutlicue [Chal-chee-oot-LEE-koo]. Ancient cultures of Mexico and Central America shared many religious beliefs and often worshiped deities with similar characteristics.

Left: In this reproduction of the mural found at the residential complex of Tepantitla, elaborately dressed priests honor the Great Goddess.

Left: The Storm God is typically represented with goggle-shaped eyes and a large upper lip, as seen in this ceramic jar.

Right: The Old God. The eyes carved on the side of the brazier are believed to be symbols of fire.

Far right: The Skinless God. This large clay sculpture was made in three pieces.

The Storm God, known as Tláloc [TLA-lok] by the Aztecs, was the second most important deity at Teotihuacán. He was the god of storms, lightning, and rain and his domain was the mountains and sky. He is often shown bringing rain by pouring water from a jar or creating lightning by hitting the jar with a spear. Both the Great Goddess and the Storm God are closely connected to water. In a society whose economy was based on agriculture, water was an essential resource.

The Storm God is depicted in several ways. In the form of a cloud he represents rainwater. The jaguar is another representation of the Storm God, perhaps because its roar sounds like the thunder that accompanies rain. In the form of a snake, the Storm God represents fertility. Depictions of snakes appear often in the art of ancient America. It was believed that each time a snake shed its skin it was born anew. Thus, it was connected to the idea of rebirth and continuity.

Another deity whose image is frequently found in the ruins of Teotihuacán is the Old God. He is usually shown in a hunched-over position supporting a brazier on his back. It is believed that the brazier was used to burn incense. In later Central American cultures this god, known as Huehuetéotl [Way-way-TAY-otl], became the center of the universe.

Two deities that represented fertility were the Fat God and the God of Spring, also known as the Skinless God or Xipe Totec [SHEE-pay TOE-tek]. Xipe Totec often appears wearing the skin of another person.

In the later years of Teotihuacán, the worship of deities related to agriculture was replaced by the worship of gods dedicated to fire, sun, and war. At this time the priests became much more militaristic and the power of religion and war became one.

The Ceremonial Center

Teotihuacán's most important religious structures were concentrated in the ceremonial center of the city, an area about two square miles in size. A long, stone walkway with buildings arranged symmetrically on either side was the main thoroughfare leading to the ceremonial center. The Aztecs named it the Avenue of the Dead because the large mounds on either side looked to them like tombs. Actually, they were the ruins of ancient temples. In Teotihuacán times, when the city was thriving, magnificent processions paraded along this wide street.

The Avenue of the Dead is 131 feet wide and, in ancient times, was more than three miles long. Today only 1.4 miles of it are visible. It runs north and south through the city, rising slightly at the north end where it stops in front of the Pyramid of the Moon. Recent mapping of the ancient city shows that there also was a main street running east from the ceremonial center and another running west. The Avenue of the Dead and these streets divide the city into four sections.

South of the Pyramid of the Sun, the San Juan River cuts across the city. Although the river is nearly dry today, it was a major source of water for the people of Teotihuacán. In ancient times, they changed its course by building a canal so that it crossed the Avenue of the Dead exactly at a right angle.

The rerouting of the river and the systematic layout of roads and buildings in Teotihuacán indicate that it was a carefully planned city. Nearly all of the buildings are aligned so that one side faces 15.5 degrees east of true north. Roads and walkways also follow this guide. Ancient priests calculated this angle by making observations of the sun and planets on special religious days. Archeologists have found circular symbols pointing both to true north and 15.5 degrees east of north carved into the floors of some buildings. These may have been surveyors' marks that were used to orient the buildings in the proper direction.

View of the Avenue of the Dead from the Pyramid of the Moon.

The Pyramid of the Moon

The Pyramid of the Moon was the first large structure built at Teotihuacán. An early version was built in the first century and then rebuilt about fifty to seventy-five years later. Then, between A.D. 150 and 225, it was enlarged again almost to the size that we see today. Its base measures 492 feet on each side and its height is 138 feet. Because the ground gradually rises toward the north end of the Avenue of the Dead, the top of the Pyramid of the Moon is at about the same level as the Pyramid of the Sun. Like the Sun pyramid, it once had a temple on its top platform.

Only the priests were allowed to climb the steep steps of the pyramids to perform their rituals and ceremonies. As at other religious centers in Central America, the temples at Teotihuacán were surrounded by large plazas and platforms. Religious ceremonies were held outdoors and the large open spaces around the sites of worship provided places where people could gather and watch.

The Pyramid of the Moon is framed by the hills of Cerro Gordo (SARE-o GORE-do) in the background. Cerro Gordo was believed to be the home of the Storm God and was sacred in Teotihuacán times.

The Pyramid of the Sun and the Pyramid of the Moon may have been dedicated to the Great Goddess and the Storm God, although it is not known which deity was associated with which pyramid. It is also believed that the tombs of the first leaders of Teotihuacán are inside the Pyramid of the Sun and the Pyramid of the Moon.

Pyramid of the Sun. A cement made from local materials holds the stones together.

The Pyramid of the Sun

The Pyramid of the Sun was constructed between A.D. 100 and 150 and then rebuilt fifty to seventy-five years later in its present form. The Pyramid of the Sun faces west and is situated so that its front faces exactly the point on the horizon where the sun sets on the days when it is at its highest point of the year. (Because Teotihuacán is south of the Tropic of Cancer, the sun is directly overhead twice a year, on May 19 and July 25.)

The base of the Pyramid of the Sun is square and measures 738 feet on each side. The pyramid's present height is 210 feet, or about as tall as a fifteen-story building. In ancient times, when a temple stood on its peak, it would have been 249 feet tall. The Pyramid of the Sun dwarfs all the surrounding structures and dominates the city. It is the largest pyramid in the world except for the pyramid at Cholula, Mexico, built around the same time, and the pyramid of Cheops in Egypt.

The Pyramid of the Sun is a solid structure consisting of a series of platforms of decreasing size built on top of one another. The slanted sides of each platform that are visible today were part of the interior structure in ancient times. When the pyramid was built, its stone walls were covered with smooth plaster which was then painted, probably red and white. In ancient times, with its colored walls looming above the horizon, the huge pyramid must have been an impressive sight to pilgrims approaching the city from afar.

The stairway to the top of the Pyramid of the Feathered Serpent is lined with carved stone heads. In ancient times, they were brightly painted.

The Pyramid of the Feathered Serpent

Around the year A.D. 150, the ruler of Teotihuacán embarked on a grand building project in the area south of the Pyramid of the Sun. Around a space bigger than thirty football fields, he built a huge, broad wall topped by fifteen small temples. (When the Spaniards first saw the wall they thought it looked like a fortress and called it the Citadel. There is no evidence, however, that it was ever used for defense by the people of Teotihuacán.)

The Citadel surrounds the third and smallest pyramid of Teotihuacán, the Pyramid of the Feathered Serpent. (The Aztec word for the feathered serpent was Quetzalcóatl [Kayt-zal-KO-atl].) It may be that the feathered serpent, a mythological creature which appears often in the art of this region, was a symbol of rulership. The Pyramid of the Feathered Serpent is lavishly decorated with large stone heads, each weighing more than four tons. The pyramid was built in two stages, the second on top of the first. The newer larger pyramid covered up and helped to preserve the artwork on the older pyramid.

Archeologists believe that the ruler who built the Pyramid of the Feathered Serpent may have been buried there, but the ruler's tomb has not been found. In other tombs inside the pyramid, though, more than one hundred skeletons have been discovered. Many of the skeletons have their hands crossed behind their backs as if they had been tied. Unlike most other human remains found at Teotihuacán, these skeletons suggest that these people were sacrificed, perhaps in honor of the gods or upon the death of the ruler. At about this time in the history of Teotihuacán, the main religious practices shifted from an emphasis on the creation myth to a cult of war and sacrifice. As in other ancient cultures of this region, blood-letting rituals and human sacrifice apparently played an important role in the religious practices of the people of Teotihuacán.

Reproduction of scaly serpent head from the Pyramid of the Feathered Serpent.

Trade and Commerce

On the west side of the Avenue of the Dead, across from the Citadel, there is a large area known as the Great Compound. In Teotihuacán times, it probably was used as an open-air market. The platforms on either side may have been where the administrative offices of the city were located. Unlike other ceremonial centers in ancient America, which were used only for religious purposes, Teotihuacán was also a center for trade and politics. It was located along a major trade route between the Gulf Coast to the east and Central Mexico to the west. Traders exported from Teotihuacán goods such as obsidian, ceramics, cloth, and products made from maguey (a plant used for its strong fibers, sharp spines, and sweet juice). They brought back cacao beans, tropical feathers, copal (a substance that was burned for incense), and other things that the people of Teotihuacán needed.

One of the most important resources for people in the ancient Americas was obsidian, a hard, glass-like rock that is formed when a volcano erupts. When obsidian is shaped into a blade, it is as sharp as steel. The people of Teotihuacán used obsidian for knives, for the tips of spears and arrows, and for ceremonial objects. Several sources of this valuable material were located near Teotihuacán. Obsidian was quarried and brought to the city where craftsmen shaped it into tools, weapons, and decorative objects. The remains of nearly one hundred obsidian workshops have been found at Teotihuacán. Obsidian products made at Teotihuacán were exported throughout the region. Archeologists have also found workshops for ceramic figures, carved stone, textiles, featherwork, and other crafts. People in similar trades seemed to live close to one another in the same part of the city.

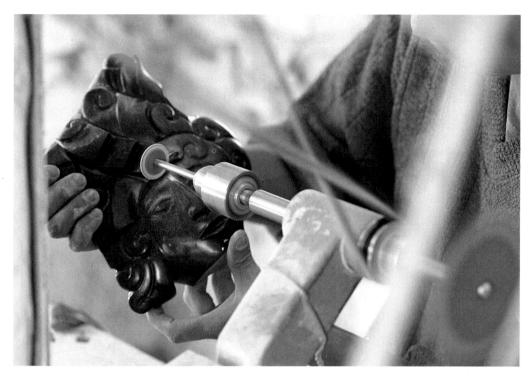

Modern obsidian carvers make figures in the style of ancient Teotihuacán.

Obsidian arrow points. The obsidian from each eruption site is unique. A technique called obsidian "finger-printing" helps archae-ologists to identify the source of the obsidian that was used to make an object.

Among the most frequently found items at Teotihuacán excavations are clay figures and pieces of pottery such as bowls, plates, and jugs. Clay was also used to make incense burners, masks, and other ceremonial items. Pottery was shaped either by hand or, in later years, in molds. Decorations on ceramics were painted, carved, or stuccoed. Clay deposits found throughout the Teotihuacán valley provided the raw material for ancient potters. The identification of different types of clay, styles of work, and methods of decoration are some of the most important ways of establishing the date and place that an item was made.

In one part of Teotihuacán, archeologists have found remains of pottery made in the style of Oaxaca [Wha-HA-ka], an area about three hundred miles to the south. This suggests that people from

Above: Cylindrical jars with three slab-shaped legs are a typical form of Teotihuacán pottery.
Below: A jaguar decorates this piece of "thin-orange" ware. This kind of pottery was a specialty of Teotihuacán.

Oaxaca lived and worked in Teotihuacán. Teotihuacán was a multiethnic city that attracted people from throughout the region.

Thousands of handmade clay figures just a few inches high have been found in the excavations at Teotihuacán. Most of these tiny figures have been found in the places where people lived. It is believed that they were used as part of daily household rituals.

Another type of object, called the puppet figurine, has movable arms and legs. No one knows why the limbs were made this way. Perhaps they were moved as part of certain religious ceremonies. Puppet figurines are found in burials so they may have been used in funeral rites.

Mysterious objects called "host" figures have also been found at Teotihuacán. These hollow clay figures have holes in their chests where other smaller figures were inserted. "Host" figures have been found in other Central American cultures as well but their meaning and use are unknown.

Above: Puppet figure.
Below: "Host" figure.

Above: Archeologists have found more masks at Teotihuacán than at any other ancient Central American site. The masks, which were made of clay or stone, were not worn, but probably used in funeral rites.

Left: Earspools.

The People of Teotihuacán

Masks, clay and stone figures, and depictions of people in murals and on pottery help us to learn what the people of ancient Teotihuacán looked like, what they wore, and some of their activities. Most of the people shown in Teotihuacán art have wide, flat foreheads. In Teotihuacán, as in other ancient cultures of the region, a wide forehead was a mark of high social status. Children of upper-class families had boards tied to the fronts and backs of their heads so that their skulls would grow into the desired shape.

Many figures in Teotihuacán. art also appear to have large, round ears. These are actually circular earrings, or earspools, which were inserted into holes in the earlobes. Other items of jewelry found at Teotihuacán include necklaces made of bones, teeth, shells, ceramics, and stone.

Small carved stone figures, like that on the right, sometimes show women wearing a type of sleeveless blouse called a "huipil" [wee-PIL], a garment still worn by some Central American people.

The type of clothing the people of Teotihuacán wore depended on their social status and activities. For ceremonies, priests often wore luxurious garments that included elaborate headdresses and highly decorated sandals. Teotihuacán soldiers wore feathered headgear and shell necklaces. The clothing of the general population of Teotihuacán was simpler. Men wore loincloths and women wore skirts and cape-like blouses. Fabric for cloth was woven from cotton, reeds, and maguey fibers. People may have worn robes made of animal skins as well. Many of the small figurines also show people with wide headbands or hat-like headdresses, which may have had religious meaning.

NORTHLAKE PUBLIC LIBRARY DISTRICT
231 NORTH WOLF ROAD
NORTHLAKE, ILLINOIS 60164

Patio of the Quetzalbutterfly palace. Carvings on the columns around the patio show a bird with butterfly wings and an obsidian eye.

Ruins of palace near the Pyramid of the Sun. The thick walls of the buildings were made of stone rubble that was then covered with concrete.

In addition to the religious and administrative buildings at the city's center, more than 4,000 other buildings made up the city of Teotihuacán. Most people lived in apartment compounds. These were large, one-story structures with small rooms opening out onto patios or covered porches that faced an inner courtyard. Narrow streets ran between the compounds, dividing the city into blocks of various sizes. Like modern cities, Teotihuacán was crowded, but the design of the housing provided a combination of privacy and fresh air.

Priests and their servants lived in beautifully decorated palaces close to the pyramids and temples. Archeologists have found the remains of nearly one hundred palaces at Teotihuacán, including one with almost three hundred rooms. One of the most beautiful, the Palace of the Quetzalbutterfly, is located on the plaza near the Pyramid of the Moon. It probably was the home of a high ranking priest. (The quetzal [KAYT-sal] is a bird native to Central America that was valued for its bright green feathers. It is frequently pictured in ancient art, often in combination with another animal such as a serpent or butterfly.)

Small shrines like this one at Atetelco were sometimes built inside the complexes where people lived. Atetelco is a residential compound located about a mile southwest of the Pyramid of the Sun.

The apartment compounds at Teotihuacán varied from sumptuous dwellings for the wealthier citizens to slumlike quarters for the poorer people. Each had fifty or more rooms and housed between sixty and one hundred people. The occupants of each compound were members of an extended family. Individual families had their own apartments with places for sleeping, cooking, eating, food storage, trash, and for performing religious rituals and funeral practices. Sometimes families shared space for keeping animals or for gathering in large groups.

Inhabitants of each apartment compound produced the stone tools, pottery, baskets, cloth, and other goods needed for daily life, but they also had specialized skills. Many were farmers who worked on the land outside the city, but others were craftsmen or workers in the building industry.

Partially restored murals on a small temple at Atetelco depict priests laden with feathers and ornaments.

This temple in the Citadel is constructed in the talud-tablero style.

Building the City

The main building materials used at Teotihuacán were stone, clay, and wood and they were worked by hand or with stone tools. The accomplishments of the people of Teotihuacán are amazing considering that they did not use metal tools or wheels or have beasts of burden to help them carry materials.

Large blocks of stone for building the pyramids and temples were cut with stone chisels from nearby quarries. The stones were dragged with ropes over hard wooden rollers to the building site and then cut precisely into the shapes that were needed.

In the early stages of Teotihuacán's development, houses were built of wood and adobe, a sun-dried mixture of clay and straw. Later, many of these were replaced by more permanent structures. Floors and the bases of walls were constructed from concrete that was made from crushed stone mixed with lime, dirt, and water. Logs cut from forests on nearby mountains were used to strengthen walls and foundations and to construct the roofs of houses.

Many of the temples were constructed in the talud-tablero [tah-LOOD ta-BLARE-o] style, an architectural technique developed by the people of Teotihuacán. First, a base was made with sloping sides (the talud), and then a platform with straight sides (the tablero) was placed on top of it. This pattern was repeated to create a series of large steps. The use of the talud-tablero style in the ceremonial centers of other cities in the region shows the wide influence Teotihuacán had on other cultures.

The outside walls of most buildings at Teotihuacán were plastered and painted. Plaster was made by burning limestone and grinding the remains into a fine powder. The powder was then mixed with sand and water to make a coating that could be smoothed over walls, floors, or roofs.

Drains and water collection containers were part of the plumbing system of Teotihuacán residences. A reservoir north of the city provided water for drinking and a sewage system.

Animals, both real and imaginary, are frequently seen in the murals of Teotihuacán.

Nearly every structure in ancient Teotihuacán was brightly painted on the outside, and many had beautiful paintings on the inside walls as well. Mural painting began in the third century A.D. Elaborate murals were painted in the temples and palaces of the priests, and the homes of the general population also had some painted decorations. Paint was made from natural dyes and applied directly onto wet plaster. Red, which signified blood and eternal life, was a predominant color. Black represented shadows and the underworld.

In many ancient cultures, including others in Mexico and Central America, rulers used art to glorify themselves. One of

Although the excavations at Teotihuacán have not yet located the ruins of a ball court, paintings such as this one from Tepantitla show that the people of ancient Teotihuacán played ball games. The curved design emerging from the player's mouth shows that he is speaking or singing.

the unusual features of the murals at Teotihuacán is that they do not depict rulers. They sometimes depict deities, priests, or processions of people, but they also contain many themes from nature. Teotihuacán art reflects the society's close connection to the natural world. Animals that appear frequently include coyotes, jaguars, pumas, owls, quetzals, doves, deer, fish, and shellfish. Although many of the mural designs are quite formal, some are more playful. Some of the murals from Teotihuacán also contain picture symbols called glyphs. These are a type of picture writing but their meaning has not yet been deciphered.

Jaguar mural located along the Avenue of the Dead.

The Fall of Teotihuacán

Teotihuacán was the largest and most important city in Mexico and Central America for more than 800 years. But around the year A.D. 750, the civilization at Teotihuacán disintegrated and the city fell into ruins. Famine, the depletion of natural resources, and a declining economy may have played a part in the fall of Teotihuacán, but archeologists believe the main cause was dissatisfaction with a government that had become increasingly oppressive. This led to a rebellion against the ruling class by the general population. In a furious uprising, the people murdered their leaders and deliberately set fire to the temples and palaces. Burn marks and layers of ashes provide evidence that there was a great fire in the ceremonial part of Teotihuacán at about this time. Without religious leaders or places to worship, the city no longer had a reason for being.

Semi-nomadic warlike groups had invaded Teotihuacán dur-

The crumbled remains at Teotihuacán are like the pieces of a giant jigsaw puzzle.

ing its last years. They adopted many of the Teotihuacán customs and artistic styles, but when the city was destroyed they left, taking with them an expert knowledge of arts and crafts. They built a new capital city at Tula, about forty miles northwest of Teotihuacán, and became known as the Toltecs, a word meaning "artist" or "artisan." The Toltec culture lasted from about A.D. 900 until 1165 when Tula was attacked by warrior tribes from the north. One of the migrating tribes that came to central Mexico at this time was that of the Mexica, or Aztec, people. In 1325 they began to build their great city, Tenochtitlán, and became the dominant culture in the region.

Even after Teotihuacán's collapse, its influence was felt in other parts of Mexico and Central America. The Toltecs continued to use some of the artistic traditions of Teotihuacán in their cities. The Aztecs also borrowed elements of Teotihuacán art and religion. When they built their Great Temple, they modeled it after the Pyramid of the Sun.

During centuries of disuse, what was left of the buildings at Teotihuacán gradually fell down and became overgrown with weeds. Their colorful murals faded and disintegrated with exposure to the weather. Objects that had been left behind were broken or buried. What we see today only hints at the greatness that was Teotihuacán.

Teotihuacán is remarkable for its monumental architecture and for the wealth of ceramics, stonework, paintings, and other artifacts that have survived to the present time. It was a highly complex society with far-reaching influence on the art, architecture, and religions of other ancient civilizations. Only a small portion of what once was Teotihuacán has been excavated. Continuing research at Teotihuacán will help us learn more about this first great city in the Americas.

Steps of the Pyramid of the Moon.

Glossary

adobe — sundried mixture of mud and straw used to make building bricks.

anthropology — the study of humankind.

archeologists — people who dig up, identify, and sometimes remove evidence of earlier cultures.

archeology — the study of a prehistoric culture by excavation and description of its remains.

artifact — humanmade object or change to the environment made by humans.

Atetelco — a richly decorated residential compound that probably belonged to a wealthy Teotihuacán family.

Avenue of the Dead — the main north-south thoroughfare in Teotihuacán.

Aztec — culture of the central plateau of Mexico; thrived from A.D. 1325 to the early 1500s.

brazier — a small container used to hold burning coals.

Chalchiutlicue — the Aztec name for the Great Goddess.

Citadel — enclosure surrounding the Pyramid of the Feathered Serpent.

copal — a resin obtained from tropical trees that was burned for incense.

Cuicuilco — ceremonial center in Mexico from about 500 to 300 B.C.

culture — people's activities as well as their clothes, food, dwellings, and beliefs.

Fat God — deity that represented fertility in Teotihuacán.

glyph — a picture symbol.

God of Spring — deity that represented fertility in Teotihuacán.

Great Compound — area on the west side of the Avenue of the Dead that may have been a marketplace and government center.

Great Goddess — the most important deity of Teotihuacán.

"host" figures — hollow ceramic figures with openings where smaller figures are inserted.

Huehuetéotl — the Aztec name for the Old God.

huipil — a sleeveless blouse worn by women in Central America.

maguey — a type of agave plant; its fibers were used as thread, its juice was made into syrup and pulque, and its pointed spines were used for bloodletting.

Maya — culture in southern Mexico and Central America; it existed from about 600 B.C. to about A.D. 900.

Náhuatl — the language of the Aztecs.

obsidian — glass-like rock formed by the eruption of a volcano.

Old God — deity of fire in Teotihuacán.

Olmec — the oldest ancient culture in Mexico; it began about 1800 B.C. and ended about 200 B.C.

Palace of the Quetzalbutterfly — palace for priests in the ceremonial center of Teotihuacán.

pulque — a fermented drink used at feasts and as a medicine.

Pyramid of the Feathered Serpent — the smallest pyramid at Teotihuacán; built in the second century A.D.

Pyramid of the Moon — the second largest pyramid at Teotihuacán; built in the first century A.D.

Pyramid of the Sun — the largest pyramid at Teotihuacán; built in the first century A.D.

quetzal — a tropical bird native to Central America.

Storm God — the second most important deity of Teotihuacán.

talud-tablero — a building style typical of Teotihuacán; it consists of a series of slanted bases topped with vertical panels.

Tenochtitlán — the capital city of the Aztecs.

Teotihuacán — an ancient culture in central Mexico that began about 150 B.C. and ended about A.D. 700.

Tepantitla — a residential compound that probably belonged to a Teotihuacán priest.

Tláloc — the Aztec name for the Storm God.

Toltec — culture on the central plateau of Mexico; existed from about A.D. 900 to 1165.

Xipe Totec — the Aztec name for the God of Spring.

Index